Serving Clients and Community through International Standards.

Quality and Environment
ISO- 9001, ISO-14001

Lisett Guevara Gulnick

SOLUTIONS

Cover design by Jim Gulnick
Cover beautification by Lisett Guevara Gulnick
www.90daysolutions.com

Photography of Lisett by Amer Chaudhry
South Jersey based photographer, available for assignments worldwide.
www.amer-fotografia.net

NEW JERSEY, U.S.A (2017)
ISBN: 978-1-941435-05-2

Published by 90daysoulmate.com, LLC

Learn how you make your book in 90 days: 90daybook.com

Table of Contents

Explore your Glass Objectives for Quality and Environment System

In this section, you can begin the first step required to establish quality and environment objectives. People have ideas to create a quality and environment system but are challenged with how to start; others have already begun, but have not established order and feel they have no control. There can be a feeling of being overwhelmed with being pulled in multiple directions, fear of committing limited resources, and apprehension of the task ahead.

In all cases, this workbook is a step-by-step guide towards making that connection between what is in the mind and heart of the leader with what it means to serve clients and community. In addition, the outcomes and results of the exercises included within provide effective actions to invigorate and enhance a thriving business.

It is possible to think, imagine, and dream about what is desired and what it would mean as a result to make it happen. If the tools to plan and implement those ideas are not available and the ability to realize these results methodically and productively are distant, then we suffer the consequences of living in a dream that in many cases may become a nightmare.

This workbook is a tool that helps you to find the necessary actions so that the thrilling ideas in your mind can be projected and brought into reality. It helps you cut through the waste, drill down to core competencies, and polish your processes. It is in the practical application of the materials provided that goals are achieved and progress is measured.

Like many other companies, you may have happened to think of ways of perfecting your business based upon the need in the market. It might have been a product or service that was not being marketed yet or at least not in the right way or to the right people. Maybe your company thought that it could enter a new market segment and successfully expand its business. How many times does a few weeks or months pass, and then you see a competitor that has already taken care of that market segment and you feel late to the table? Maybe you thought about it yourself but unfortunately took little or no action.

Perhaps you did not take action because you did not have the tools, the courage, the time, or the money. These are all powerless excuses from now. With the information in this book and the creativity of your mind, you will realize that there are no limitations in starting or expanding a business. All the limitations were only in your mind.

First you must know your mission. What did you come to do while on this planet? What is your duty in life? Do you know what talents and abilities you possess? Do you know what you are passionate about?

These questions seem easy, but we must devote the necessary time to them, so that you can connect what you are currently doing with what you want to do.

Many people have their own business for many reasons. Maybe it was a family business, they came across it without planning, they were presented with an unexpected opportunity, or because someone invited them and they found it interesting to join in the project. But, there is another group of business owners that have always had a dream. They had in their minds and hearts the hope of doing something that they loved, something they found exciting, and something they knew was their mission in life.

We will provide some tips on how to connect what you have inside with what your organization does or is required to do:

1. What are the talents, skills, and knowledge that you possess?

2. What are the things you love to do?
3. How do your talents, skills, and knowledge relate to your passion?
4. What do you believe you came to this planet to do?
5. What do you want to do in your company or project?
6. What are your personal and business needs?
7. What are your personal and business values?
8. How are your values related to your needs?

Before answering each question or investigating each subject, it is important to understand the elements that are used in this exercise. We will explain in more detail, so that you can do an excellent job of analysis and documentation. Once you have developed the answers to these questions or subjects, you will be able to have a clearer picture, and you will know whether or not your life mission can fit your business mission.

Remember something very important: when action movie heroes must fulfill their missions, they are never discouraged, they never tire, they do not complain, and they do not protest. There are no excuses or obstacles that they cannot deal with in order to fulfill their missions. And while they are confronting problems and fighting enemies, every obstacle becomes an adventure in which the hero does not give up on achieving his goal.

We invite you to discover your life mission. Put on your superhero cape to connect with yourself, and you can achieve everything you desire.

1. What are the talents, skills, and knowledge that you possess?

It is important to know the difference between these elements, because while they may look similar, they are not. Knowledge is the fact of knowing something, and skill is the ability to do it.

When we speak of knowledge, we refer to theoretical information acquired about a subject, whether it is information learned through reading, training, or any other form of education.

On the other hand, skills are the practical ability to apply the knowledge gained. In some cases skills may be innate, as there are people who have developed skills without studying previously, perhaps by watching or simply making an attempt using trial and error, and have thus developed a specific skill.

When it comes to talent, we can say it is a combination of the two definitions, where the capacity of a person to understand how to resolve situations in an intelligent way is combined with their own abilities, skills, knowledge, experience, and aptitudes.

Being able to describe every talent, skill, and knowledge you possess in clear terms will give you the basics needed to better know yourself and to understand the tools you have.

Be aware of the importance of this part of your self-analysis, since a lack of knowledge or awareness of the skills we have can make the road more difficult to navigate. And when we know who we really are, we can better understand our own strengths and weaknesses. In this way, you can identify areas that need improvement and those you can take advantage of more easily.

Imagine a person who has stage fright and is afraid of public speaking, but wishes to be a famous author, as the person has many good ideas and does not need to deal with large groups to write books. That's fine, but when it comes time to sell the book, one of the techniques is through seminars, workshops, conferences, etc. Then, that person has the option of developing a new talent or of hiring another person to do that activity.

With this example, we are not saying that the fact of not having specific knowledge and/or a certain skill will limit you in completing your project or life mission. What we want to explain is that by recognizing who you are, you will more clearly understand your advantages and disadvantages when it comes to establishing your mission in life.

When people recognize their talents, they can become superheroes more quickly and easily. Some people have an innate ability to connect with others when communicating, and they can sell just about anything because they have that gift that makes them unique when presenting a product or service. Such people can go far in the areas where they recognize their own abilities, because just knowing what talents they have and above all, believing in their own talents, gives them the potential they need to succeed.

A simple way to perform this analysis is to recall some activities in which you have easily succeeded, and where other people have recognized that you have performed very well.

Another way is to evaluate the knowledge gained during all the years you have lived, as well as the experience you have gained. There are people who have worked for twenty years as assistants or technicians in a machine shop and do not recognize all the knowledge they have in the mechanical or electrical areas, their knowledge of parts, the amount of training they have received, etc.

Evaluate yourself and be thorough in reviewing your entire path, both in knowledge and in talent, and design a comprehensive document that illustrates who you really are and what you really have. At the end of the chapter you can use the form **"Determine Your Skills"**.

2. What are the things you love to do?

Recognizing the things we are passionate about is an interesting task. We will take you by the hand to discover the activity that moves the fiber of your being, the activity you can perform with excitement, focus and energy. We recommend, as with all the activities in this book, that you take notes, that you write, because through writing you can tap the wealth of information that you must organize and process in order to put it into action.

The best way to discover your passion is to answer the following questions:

- Which activity makes time pass so that you do not realize it?
- What would you be willing to do without being paid a cent?
- At this moment, what would you choose to do for the rest of your life?
- If you died and had the opportunity to return, what would you do?
- Which activities trigger your creativity and excite you?

- Recall moments when you do something that brings joy, makes you jump up and down, energizes you and brings you happiness.

Once you answer these questions honestly, you will be more focused on the path you want to follow. Take your time when answering these questions, because ideas will surface in your mind and can revive your passion.

3. How do you relate your talents, skills, and knowledge to your passion?

In this step of the exercise it is important that you have written the answers to steps one and two, because now you need to relate your passion to your skills, talents and knowledge.

The best way to do this is to make a comparison chart where you list your knowledge, skills, abilities, talents, and the activities that thrill you. In this way, you will be able to connect what they have in common and what you can best use to turn your passion into action. Having a passion without taking action turns into frustration, and it does a lot of damage over the years if it is not fulfilled. So you see the importance of this activity to your personal life as well as your business, financial, family, and professional lives. Here you can discover what's happening in your life that is causing you not to succeed in what you really want.

You may be reading this book and looking at the exercises and thinking, *I don't have time to answer, let alone write the answers to this many questions; I need to solve my business problem, my financial problem.* Consequently, you do not follow the steps listed here, and later you might wonder why you are in the same place as before, why you do not advance in business.

Observe whether following instructions is a problem for you, since in most cases this is the greatest obstacle to improving any area of your life.

Having identified the resources available to you when setting up a business is a priority, and one of the main resources is the business knowledge that you must establish. Imagine that you are going to install a laboratory for stem cells taken from the placentas of babies at birth, but you do not have the slightest idea of how to do this or what benefits it has, and you do not even like medicine. You are trying to develop something for which motivation and enthusiasm will not guarantee that you are on the right track, unless you are simply an investor in the business.

The analysis of this activity should highlight those cases that are related, and you must find out which passions have no relation to your talents. In this way you will either make the decision to work and develop new talent, or simply to dedicate yourself only to the activities that you are passionate about and for which you have the talent, knowledge, and skills.

You must be honest with yourself and not hide your conflicting activities, as this is where energy is dissipated and where lack of productivity demolishes projects, plans, and passions.

4. What do you believe you came to this planet to do?

It may seem a little strange to ask what you came to this planet to do, but this kind of question gives us the introspection to analyze our life mission, the reason and the cause for being here with the skills and talents we possess. In addition to the knowledge gained on the way, this mix of who you are and what your goal is opens doors in your mind through which you can see answers that are often very obvious, but cannot be seen.

Describe in detail the reason why you are here in this place, country, city, community where you belong, with the cargo of information and knowledge that you have.

Starting to write about this will allow you to take the first steps to identify your mission in life. And then you must link your mission in life to the mission of your business.

We will help you with some personal questions so that you have the foundation that will facilitate the realization of the organization's mission. You cannot disassociate the two missions because that will not allow you to understand the fundamental reason for the business you are establishing.

The following example will show you how to connect the information to create a mission for your organization.

In Lisett's case, she has a natural talent for negotiation; her passion for finding out how to proactively unite resources with needs makes her an expert negotiator. Additionally, she has trained for many years as an information engineer, with a master's degree in industrial engineering, which gives her the tools to manage information, processes, innovation, and technology, among others. Based on these elements and her passion for creating solutions, she established the company *90Daysolutions Llc*, which offers consulting services, training, and business reengineering.

The mix of knowledge, skills, and experience that she possesses means that her **life mission** combined with the mission of the organization work together for a common goal. And when we determine with whom we are working, we open up opportunities to clearly see our potential customers.

Questions:

- What do we do well as people?
- What are we seeking with what we do?
- Where do we do it?
- Why do we do it?
- Who do we do it for?

Answering these questions in a personal manner allows you to combine this information with your business activities, and this is good because these same questions will later be applied to identify the mission of your business.

Your personal mission can be described in one or more phrases; in just answering these questions, you will recognize what your mission in life is, and what you came to do here on this planet.

Do not be surprised if in doing this exercise you discover new things, new ideas, and even new ways different from those you previously considered or have been using in your current business. This is the time to discover yourself and the talents you can put into action as a driving force to achieve your desired success.

Humans redesign themselves constantly; you can re-create, re-start yourself. Allow yourself the opportunity to start a new project, a new lifestyle, a new season, a refresh of your daily life. No matter how old you are, allow this change in your life, because we do not know what will happen in the next.

5. What do you want to do in your company or project?

At this point, with all the personal details, we can focus the artillery on your business. Does the project you are working on, or the company where you are working, allow you to fulfill your mission in life?

The company for which you want to develop a mission and vision must have the service and/or product it offers identified. No matter what type of organization you have, the important thing is to specifically describe what it is dedicated to, and then you will be able to determine what it does in comparison with what it wants to do.

The mission of an organization is a public announcement, which should be visible to everyone and especially kept in view of the owners of the organization, its employees, its customers, its suppliers, and the general public.

It is this flag that symbolizes power, choice, clarity, focus, direction, order, and why not say it, the feeling of defiance, of challenges. It is the announcement to the entire world that <u>we know who we are and where we are going</u>.

When organizations know, understand, feel, breathe, and vibrate recognizing <u>who they are</u> and <u>where they are going</u>, the energy that moves them is much better, and their productivity is shown by the facts.

Develop your business mission.

To design the mission of the organization, you must simply answer the same questions as in point four, but with a focus on your business or project.

Below, we pose these questions again with a business approach, so that you may describe the mission of the company. The wording of a mission statement has been a topic of discussion for many years among business consultants, business owners, auditors, etc. But the way you draw it up is not important here; what matters is the information it contains. This is why we recommend that you write it with the information we have asked, and another important point is its publication.

Questions:
- What do we do well as a company?
- What are we seeking with what we do?
- Where do we do it?
- Why do we do it?
- Who do we do it for?

You can find a lot of information on the internet about how to write a mission statement, but the bottom line here is that it contains clear information about what the company does, how it does it, why it does it, and for whom. This is the foundation for realizing the vision.

Develop your business vision.

When you were answering the questions above, you may have listed activities that you are not currently doing and that should wait a little longer to be implemented in your business plan, either in the medium or long term. That declaration of aspiration about what you envision and desire for your company's future is what you are going to develop into a business vision.

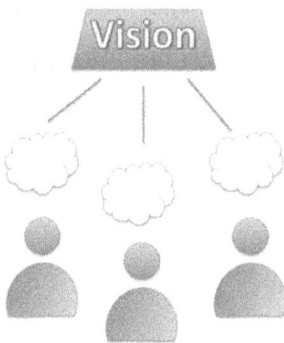

The important thing is to recognize and differentiate between what you are and do (mission) and what you want to be and want to do (vision). Putting these two statements together allows you to create a future plan. It is the ability to know where you stand and which way you will lead the organization.

Most things in life were first created mentally, then were visualized and put on paper, and finally created physically. The power to visualize becomes the strategy of creation for organizations. Creative visualization consists in having an image of what you want for the organization, and this image is recreated in the minds of the participants in the project or business. It is done in such a way that each person is involved in an exchange of ideas about how they want to project the organization into the future, and when they have all shared their input, it is captured on paper to make it easier to establish goals and plans to achieve them.

In designing the vision it is advisable to involve project members and other stakeholders, because the point of view of a third party often helps create fresh ideas that benefit the new vision of the organization.

Grounded with mission information that has already been developed, you can generate new ideas and help yourself with the following questions:

- What is the desired image of our business?
- How will we be in the future?
- What will we do in the future?
- What activities will we develop in the future?

Once you have established the mission and vision, it will be easier to establish the objectives and the organizational structure -- in short, what you want to do and who you are going to do it with.

6. What are your personal and business needs?

You have probably heard of Maslow's famous pyramid that describes the hierarchy of human needs. This pyramid is very simple and shows levels of needs ranging from basic to high-level. This scale has a logical reason to exist, and satisfying the needs at each level allows you to attempt to achieve the next higher level. Likewise if a lower level need becomes unmet, the upper level needs that have been achieved may become threatened. A strong foundation is therefore necessary in maintaining a full and satisfying life balance between your business and personal needs.

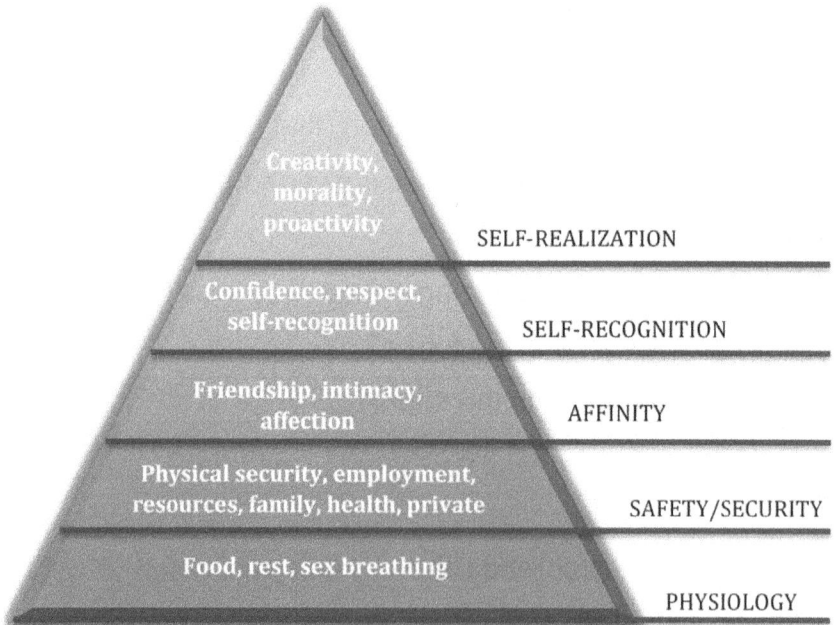

Creativity, morality, proactivity — SELF-REALIZATION

Confidence, respect, self-recognition — SELF-RECOGNITION

Friendship, intimacy, affection — AFFINITY

Physical security, employment, resources, family, health, private — SAFETY/SECURITY

Food, rest, sex breathing — PHYSIOLOGY

The hierarchy of needs is critical for understanding certain details that can derail your business, and even derail your 90-day project.

If the basic needs of food, health, and safety are not covered, it is very difficult for human beings to generate new ideas, apply creativity, and take on major new challenges.

We have touched on this theory of the hierarchy of needs because we can use this classification to help you determine your personal needs and the needs of your business.

As you can see, all the information we are giving you is linked and has a logical sequence that allows you to establish a system with solid and sustainable foundations. Relating your personal mission to the mission of the organization lets you see you are walking down the right path, and linking your individual needs with business needs allows you to direct the path to the desired and necessary objectives.

Make a list of the personal needs that you have at this time; you can use the picture of the pyramid, where you can go from eating and resting, through security, affection, and trust, to reach self-actualization. Once you write the list, it is important that you arrange it based on your priorities, so that the items are in order from highest to lowest priority according to their importance.

Then make a list of the organization's needs, and similarly, list them from most to least important. Once both lists are complete, select the top three needs from both lists and check whether or not they are similar.

This exercise will show you whether there is affinity in terms of the needs of both areas so that you can determine whether the objectives that you must contemplate are going in the same direction.

Needs are responsible for *activating emotions* that can inspire or destroy a business. Emotions are an important factor that many entrepreneurs manage wisely, and give them a role in making decisions that can cause them to win or lose. When needs are aligned with values and do not contradict them, harmony appears and the forces of resistance are minimized.

7. What are your personal and business values?

Values exist in homes, families, and society, as well as in businesses and organizations. Values are fundamental beliefs that characterize human beings when they think, choose, and act at any given time. Values are the thermometer of our behavior, and form a pattern of behavior within each of our personal, family, social, and work circles. When values are clearly defined and established, it is easier to understand the causes and reasons for people's behavior in any situation.

There are people who are so grounded in their values that their decisions are based purely on the pattern of their beliefs, whether or not those decisions are beneficial for themselves or their environment. That pattern is the lens through which you see the world and through which your interpretation of the world will also be based.

In organizations, values have been pillars that have sustained businesses for many years. There are companies that have very well-founded values despite conflicting values held by the society around them, or by their workers or employees, or by the country where the business is established. As long as the values are well-founded they may guarantee the integrity of the organization. It is amazing how we have known companies that have gone through economic, social, and political crises and have maintained strong values in order to be a center of transformation for persons belonging to the organization.

The point of this discussion is to understand that personal values are not contrary to organizational values. To simplify, we will present an example: let's assume that the members of an organization have the value of honesty as number one on their list of values, but have created an organization whose main customer is the government of a country where corruption levels are very high. When presenting their product or service to their unique customer, they must act in opposition to the principal value of the organization. At that moment, they must make the decision to change the focus of the company to the private sector where this value is not affected, because functioning in a manner contrary to the values of the organization will sooner or later destroy it.

You can see why it is in your best interests to establish a list of your personal values and your organizational values, and handle these in the same way as you did the needs. List the values in descending order, and compare the first three values in each list. In this way, you can observe and manage information so that both lists can operate in synchrony and not create conflicts, which we often think are simple but can become a silent enemy that eventually explode and destroy the organization or its members. That's when illnesses and stress arise, and the business becomes a disagreeable place where you feel obligated to be and where it is not pleasant to work.

8. How are your values related to your needs?

When making your lists of both values and needs, detailed analysis is required to establish whether any of your personal or organizational needs connect in a positive or negative way with the values.

Let's start with the values and what we will call anti-values. This refers to those values that were programmed into our minds and our beliefs in a positive way, but the way they have been interpreted has generated a negative aspect that allows them to be called anti-values.

To better explain the point we present the following example: when a father and mother tell their children that "*big boys don't cry*", with this they are seeking to form a value of strength, of having the maturity to face things in a brave way, but at the same time this phrase expresses a limitation of feelings and emotions. Consequently, these children connect in their minds that the fact of expressing their emotions makes them weak, and then they close up and will not share their feelings and experiences, blocking an emotional area; and they think that the less they feel, the better.

It is therefore important to examine the values we have created in our minds and our organizations with phrases that can be interpreted negatively, which may in turn lead to conflicts with the needs of the organization or its members.

There are values that can falter in the presence of some needs; and that's where this chapter of the book seeks to make a great contribution to the reader, because a business owner may have strong values based on not asking for help, not accepting cash or credit, but the organization needs funding to continue operating. This is where the values should be revised, because as an organizational objective the company must generate revenues and profits, and this sort of value may be blocking the progress of the organization in some cases, or may be taking care of or protecting the organization in other cases.

This is a very interesting and delicate area where with the help of developed documents, analysis meetings, and interpretation, you can understand which aspects are holding back the growth of your organization or placing it at risk.

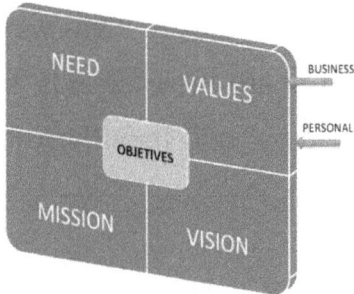

In the adjacent table, it is important to note that the mission, vision, and values all need to be reviewed in a personal and organizational manner in order to set clear and achievable targets.

GOALS

Goal setting is a key task in which we must consider certain basic premises in order to declare, implement, measure, and fulfill objectives.

Goals are established objectives that must be achievable, measurable, and understandable. Above all, goals must have people who are responsible for them. We have encountered organizations that have very well-designed mission statements along with infallible measurement and monitoring methods, but which are weak in that the people responsible for the activities needed to meet objectives are not clearly identified.

This is where a common goal found throughout the organization, such as customer care, becomes a mystery distributed among everyone, without a leader or person responsible for the measurement or fulfillment of that goal.

When you set goals, it is because you have already defined where the organization is going. Therefore it is very important to know the mission and vision, because that is the basis from which you design activities, tasks and actions that allow you to achieve the objectives.

Goals should have the following elements:
1. Describe what is to be achieved in a clear, simple, and understandable way.
2. Set a goal for which the achievement of the objective can be measured.
3. Declare a term, period, or time for the accomplishment.
4. Establish a leader and people responsible for the objectives.
5. Set periods of evaluation and measurement of the objectives.

6. Perform monitoring with the established method or pattern of measurement.

7. Compare with previous measurements, and analyze behavior.

8. Create adjustments and methods for improving compliance.

9. Document all the steps above to create the records necessary to enable you to show the progress, compliance, and monitoring of your organization's system.

CHEW™ Analysis

AREA	CONFIDENCE	HESITATION	EXCITEMENT	WORRY
CHEW™ Analysis Confidence, Hesitation, Excitement, Worry				
Customer Services	Order speed	Software not strong	Customer Satisfaction	Cost involved
	Understand Customer requirement			

OBJECTIVES-TARGETS- PROGRAMS

REVIEW DATE:

OBJECTIVE DESCRIPTION	TARGET DESCRIPTION (Timeline + Goal)	Unit of Measuring	PROGRAM IN PLACE	Frecuency review	PROCESS	RESP. DEPT.

Risk Assessment in the Glass Market

It is necessary for any type of organization to know and manage risks in its processes, activities, services, products, and staff. Many people know and talk about business risks, but very few know how to manage them. Risks often seem as if anything can happen, but most people think that nothing will ever happen to them; moreover, people try not to think about risks, believing that if they think and imagine the risks they will appear, as in a ritual where "bad luck" is invoked. These people believe that if they start thinking something will happen to the organization, the chances of it happening will increase.

We can assure you that not thinking about risks does not make them go away. The existence of risk in every activity you do in life is real. And not foreseeing the existence of risk puts you and the organization in a more vulnerable position. The point is that you can minimize, control, transform, and eventually eliminate the risk when it is evaluated, treated, monitored, and managed. Well-handled risk management guarantees a beneficial impact on the probability of the risk's occurrence and materialization, and it doesn't just help to control it. Risk management will improve the organization's strategies and effective decision-making. It will help with change management and increase operational efficiency, as well as providing other benefits such as cost reduction, competitive advantage, better market presence, and even a better image as an organization in the community.

Principles of risk management

Risk management is a systematic process that is supported by a number of principles. These principles form the pillars which support the structure of the organization under an internal and external focus. For the design of risk management, it is necessary to know the size of the organization, its nature and complexity, the scope of its activities, and its limitations not only in terms of its internal management but also external aspects that may affect it, whether legal, regulatory, government, financial, social, etc.

For profound risk management, it is necessary to know the governing principles:

1. The design of risk management should create value for the organization, assisting with legal, financial, quality, safety, health, and environmental management, among others.

2.   Risk management should be part of the existing organizational processes, and should not be seen as an additional control, but should be immersed in each of the existing processes and activities.

3. When establishing the criteria to be controlled, they must permit easy decision-making by the organization's directors.

4. There should be a specific focus on managing uncertainties, and how to take action to control them.

5.   Risk management should be designed under a systems approach, where each of the parts is linked and results can be measured to confirm reliability.

6. Monitor the best information that goes into the processes such as experience, observation, analysis, and expert recommendations, so that the information is dealt with in terms of risk management.

7. The design must be made to fit the organization, structured by the type and scope of its specific risk profile.

8.   Management should take into account the human and cultural aspects related to the organization, both in the outside environment and within internal management.

9. The information used in management should be transparent and open so that stakeholders have access to the information.

10. The risk management system should be dynamic, interactive, and responsive to change. Keep the information updated, and monitor the constant exchange between events and the information provided.

11. The organization should ensure the implementation of continuous improvement strategies, based on risk detection, analysis, and implementation of improvement actions.

Risk Assessment

This consists of identifying risks, followed by evaluating or classifying them. To create a detailed risk assessment, we will provide the necessary tools for designing your risk management system. Remember that every risk management system is tailored to suit the organization, but what we offer here is a generic model, and the details of adjustment must be developed for you and your team. If you have the chance to get an expert in the area to help you in the use of risk assessment, it is recommended that you do it, because here you are playing with elements of supreme importance to your organization.

The goal of offering you the "**Risk Assessment**" form is to allow you to record information in a table or spreadsheet that will be easy to look at, since you will structure it for processes or activities, thus allowing it to sweep through every area of the organization. Although a simple description of a risk is sometimes enough, there are circumstances where detailed description of the risks may be required in order to provide a holistic view of the evaluation process.

See how interesting it is to be able to weigh a risk, to manage it, and to know which risks are more likely than others and what kind of impact they can have on the organization. Risks can be quantitative or qualitative in terms of their probability of occurrence and their potential consequences or impacts. The organization needs to develop its own methodology for measuring the likelihood of the risk. A simple evaluation method might be to multiply the threat by the vulnerability.

Let's define each term:

Risk: The combination of the probability of an event's occurrence and its consequences.

Threat: The dangerous condition that can cause the risk; determined by its intensity and frequency.

Vulnerability: The characteristics and circumstances that make the organization susceptible. Vulnerability is composed of exposure, susceptibility and resistance to adaptation to effects.

RISK = THREAT x VULNERABILITY

TYPES OF THREATS
- Natural disasters (floods, earthquakes, hurricanes, etc.).
- Human (lack of staff, poor maintenance, management error).
- Technology (equipment failure, lack of connectivity).
- Security (physical, personal, financial, social).
- Deliberate or intentional.

Threats can be classified from very low, low, medium, and high to very high, and can be characterized with numbers, for example 1 to 5.

TYPES OF VULNERABILITY
- Lack of knowledge.
- Fraud.
- Loss of assets.
- Loss of staff.
- Theft of products.
- Decomposition of raw materials.

The vulnerability may vary depending on the type of business and process you are evaluating. We have simply listed a few examples so you can have an idea of risk management in your organization.

These can also be classified from very low, low, medium, and high to very high, and can be characterized with numbers from 1 to 5.

Management of the risk assessment table

For the design of the risk assessment, follow these steps:

STEP 1: The first column of the table shows the name of the **activity to be evaluated**. You can guide yourself with your list of processes and procedures for the area and select the activities that you are interested in evaluating.

STEP 2: Determine the **nature of risk**. Here is where you develop the possibilities of risks that this activity can incur. You can have more than one type of risk associated with this activity.

STEP 3: The **frequency** with which the activity is performed. Here you should write whether the activity is done daily, weekly, biweekly, monthly, or as often as it is done in the organization. This will help you determine whether the threat is high or not.

STEP 4: Indicate the **threat** presented by this activity as a number, according to the scale determined by the organization.

STEP 5: Indicate the **vulnerability** involved in this activity as a number, according to the scale determined by the organization.

STEP 6: Multiply the number in the threat box by the number in the vulnerability box, and write the resulting number in the **risk index**.

STEP 7: The **type of control** to be applied, whether to minimize the risk, transfer it, tolerate it with controls, treat it to modify its source, or eliminate it. Remember that when the risk index is high, more attention must be paid to the implementation of controls.

STEP 8: Describe **the actions** required to accomplish whatever was determined in the previous box as the type of control to be applied.

STEP 9: The **person responsible** for maintaining risk control and the actions. Here you put the name of the person responsible for controlling the assessed risk.

With the development of this table, you can administer practical and secure risk control that will give you more peace of mind at the moment of any contingency, as well as providing you with a decision-making tool. Developing the entire picture with each of the key activities of the organization may be tedious work, but it is worth the trouble when you and your team look at each activity and visualize the inherent risks that you have as an organization.

MONITOR THE RISK

To accomplish monitoring, it is necessary to implement the techniques provided in the list of the principles of risk management, where you take care of management tracking, linking people in the organization, as well as the control and use of information to generate a continuous improvement system.

If you established goals in the action plan that you designed in the risk assessment table, this will let you know what level of risk is involved in a certain activity, and how it has improved over time with implementation of the proposed actions. If you do not see improvements, this justifies the recurring review of the table so that it contains an action or group of actions that will improve the process and minimize or eliminate the assessed risk.

You see how interesting the proper use of this technique is, and the benefits it can give you when you apply a **system of business risk management**. Here we list some of the benefits you will get:

- Creation of risk management awareness in the organization.
- Compliance with legal and regulatory requirements, as well as any customer requirements.
- Continuous business improvement.
- Establishment of a reliable method for decision-making.
- Improvement of incident prevention and management.
- Loss minimization.
- Improved management of leadership objectives.
- Improved trust in employees, customers, and suppliers.
- Improved management of the organization's internal information.
- Increased safety in general.
- Creation of a proactive culture, rather than a reactive culture.
- Improved identification of opportunities and threats.
- Better management of resources.
- Creation of a culture of prevention.

RISKS ASSESSMENT

ACTIVITY	NATURE OF RISK	FREQUENCY	THREAT	VULNERABILITY	RISK INDEX	TYPE OF CONTROL	ACTIONS	RESPONSIBLE

Do-it-yourself Business and Basic Marketing Strategy

The accelerated pace of technology requires that we develop skills to make inroads into a changing society, where markets must move very quickly and in the right direction. In global trade, you must adapt your product or service to various sectors, groups, or markets. However, these different groups see you and your organization as a single image under a digital interface -- your website - which can be visited worldwide. You must be able to manage this digital portal intelligently, because the dream of bringing in millions of customers via global access to your company can become a sad reality where your website has few or no visitors, let alone sales.

That feeling of believing that we could be visited by millions and millions of people, and that most of those people could be our customers, is an exciting sensation that can either finish with a happy ending, or turn into a worse nightmare than we ever imagined.

As entrepreneurs, we must have vision and enthusiasm to act quickly but with patience, and with a strategic and innovative focus that helps us move forward without wasting resources. It is amazing how human beings act in times of scarcity and of plenty. In times of scarcity, we act shrewdly to conserve resources; in times of abundance, we grow slow and confident that things will stay the way they are. The same thing happens when we enter technological society. It provides so many data resources, information, and access methods that we start feeling too secure, and we submerge ourselves in all this data and access without getting effective results.

We are now short of time in an environment where information and opportunities are abundant. It is important to discover the new skills that we must develop to survive.

Advertising

We attended a business meeting at the Chamber of Commerce. Most participants were owners of small and medium-sized businesses. The topic under discussion was advertising and marketing. This question arose: "What is the most effective way to get good publicity?" That gave rise to a discussion, and these comments were heard:

- "People do not pay attention to newspapers or radio."
- "I invested money in a website and paid for a number of social media memberships, and I have seen no results."

- "I have a contract with an advertising and marketing company that sends monthly bills, but I don't see the number of customers in my business growing."

These were the statements of some of the disgruntled businessmen we met. It was a stampede of negativity, one right after the other. There seemed to be no escape. It was like a virus that spread in the meeting room, and it was as if no antidote could cure the disease. The speakers identified others who were responsible and could be blamed, such as the economy, the government, society, and the country.

The Vaccine for the Virus

When they have good print or radio advertising, or even a good ad on a billboard, many business owners think they have paid the necessary marketing costs.

A customer may arrive and enter your business; but if your customers do not return, it shows that advertising, no matter how cost-effective and striking, only inspires the first visit of a client. In many cases the client may not return, because there is no need, or because the client is unhappy. The second reason will cause greater losses because a bad review of a business multiplies quickly and exponentially, especially today with the use of technology and social networking. This will make it very difficult to get back an unhappy customer, or to attract potential future customers.

When was the last time you saw a repeat customer in your business? When was the last time a customer recommended your business to a friend?

Advertising by Word of Mouth
One of the most effective forms of advertising is word of mouth. Your business must create such a unique and profound experience that your client cannot resist telling a friend. If your company does not respond with intensity to its target market, and does not make people feel they must tell others about your business, you are wasting your time on marketing and advertising, and must drastically change your business vision.

The business owners who made the comments above suffered losses because they relied solely on advertising to attract customers. They did not believe in, or did not know about, word-of-mouth advertising. They thought advertising could make up for what was missing in their businesses.

If you manage to convince a person to enter your business by a means such as marketing, how can you ensure that person will return?

Ask yourself the following questions to see if you have the knowledge and behavior that encourages good word of mouth.

- Do you know how you can have an impact on your customers?
- Do you know how to measure weekly customer traffic, and whether or not the same customers return?
- Do you know your customers' expectations?
- Do you know when a customer is unhappy?

If you can guarantee you will impress your customers, and that they will recommend your business to their acquaintances, then we guarantee you will succeed. We can also guarantee that your ads will start working for you. However, remember that advertising does not do all the work for you; it only does the initial work. After that, your product or service must ensure your success.

Word of mouth is like a live, walking advertisement with emotions that connects with hundreds and thousands of people, who become a network of potential customers to whom information is sent personally.

Creating word-of-mouth advertising may not require you to significantly increase your investment in your business. Instead of spending all your money on newspaper ads, trade shows, events, radio stations, websites, and cable TV promotions, put your money directly into your business, so you can create in your specific market an experience that leads customers to speak well of your business.

Personalized Invitation

Let's imagine two friends are in a shopping mall. As good friends, they know each other's tastes. One tells the other about a clothing store selling new pants that her friend would like; she describes the colors, patterns, and fabrics; the excellent customer service; the comfortable dressing rooms; the discount coupons. She is playing with her friend's emotions, and so her friend feels as if she must buy pants at that store.

If a potential customer asks somebody about a specific business because of a need to buy something, that we can not call word-of-mouth advertising. Real word of mouth creates a personalized invitation only when a client feels excited and driven to tell someone else about your business.

You cannot control people outside your business. You can only control what happens within your business. Your main objective is to change your business so that it leaves such a deep and lasting impression on your customers, they must tell someone else.

And take care, because as potent and powerful as this tool is to create customer loyalty and attract a group of fans, it can also cause loss of customers and bad reputation.

The franchise opportunity

There are various franchises in different types of markets, but the main value in franchises is in standardization and processes: how to open and close the store; how to decorate; how to display the merchandise; how employees should dress, behave and speak; how to cook; how to deliver a product; and how to measure service quality.

No matter what type of business you have, you can provide a customer with the same experience as a franchise, or close. You must give your customers a repeatable experience. They need to know what to expect from your business. They should have the same experience whenever they visit, and feel that you treat all customers equally.

Customer-focused service lies in the act of positioning your business to think about the customer as its principal objective. Design your processes, structures, products, and services with a customer focus. This seems logical to many, but we are sometimes amazed to observe during an evaluation how a company has designed its processes, products, and services in such a way as to make the customer suffer.

For example, a company sells a number of products for the home online. When a customer wishes to return a product, the steps or processes are designed so that:

- It will cost the customer more to ship the product than the product is worth.
- The product quality is bad; international shipping is paid by the customer, and the customer will only be refunded 40% of the original value.
- When a customer writes to the company, no answer is made until a week later, or perhaps ever.

This kind of business does not have customer-focused processes. Its processes are geared to sell once, with no thought towards encouraging a second sale.

Therefore, it is very important to review your business processes, perhaps with the help of a third party. Many business owners believe they are focused on meeting the needs of their customers, but this is just a delusion or a fantasy.

First visualize the target, and then shoot

If you open a business to satisfy your reasoning or your tastes, you are on your way to a battle that will be difficult, or that you may lose. But if you build your business based on a specific market, identifying what this market needs and what you can offer it, assessing whether the market has access to your business and the money to pay, then you are on the way to competition. If you can focus on the target market and also create a unique and incredible emotional experience, you are on the road to victory.

We will give you the following basic tips to achieve this:

- Keep your focus on the target.
- Observe the market reality with objectivity.
- Refine and update processes to match changes in the environment.
- Maintain a franchise philosophy in which the treatment of all customers is alike and repetitive.
- Be persistent and consistent in creating an environment where customers and employees are passionate about what they get and what they give.

In this way you will understand that having a global business vision allows you to see beyond a simple failure of marketing and advertising, and will open the door to sustained success without large investments of money, knowledge, and action.

Notes:

Strategies for Turning your Customers into Partners

Target Market

What is your target market? If you own a coffee shop, is it people who drink coffee?

When we talk about a target market, many people only think about the direct customer, which is fine. But we must widen our focus to a more comprehensive and global vision; that is, to see the environment that surrounds our goal.

The idea is to *minimize effort and multiply resources*. When you learn to observe the infinite resources available in the environment and to connect them with the infinite possibilities that the universe offers, you succeed in minimizing effort and creating a profound use of resources, resulting in a greater ability to penetrate the market.

We will explain this with the following example: in a store that sells video games, the target market is young people of perhaps eight to twenty years old, predominantly male, and advertising focuses exclusively on that group. But this advertising does not extend the scope of vision to what we call the second level. This second level is to think about who else can buy the products, and what ways can be used to attract more groups of customers. In this case, the strategy will be to seek to attract the parents of these young men and motivate them with the idea that they too can play with their children; in the final analysis, it is really they who pay the money so the customer can buy the product.

On the other hand, the seller can look for ways in which these potential customers are associated in order to capture groups. For example, it could be sports teams: a promotion of video games related to baseball, directed at students who play on baseball teams. It is this openness of ideas that will improve vision and market penetration.

Once the seller has determined what this group (which in this case would be coaches and school teachers) is looking for, a campaign can be prepared and aimed at this sector or group which will generate more associations, and could be copied to use for another group of potential customers at the second level.

Four Steps to Developing your Target Market

When we look at this example, we can determine several important features to keep in mind for the development of the target market. The essence of these features can be discovered through the following **four steps**:

1. Identification of the principal market segment.
2. Identification of the second-level market segment.
3. Identification of possible ways of associating groups of potential customers.
4. Development of campaigns aimed at different levels and groups in a standard way that can be repeated, optimizing resources.

STEP 1: Main Market

How can you do this? How can you put your business down on paper and generate a methodical plan that lets you view and open your vision of the target market at different levels?

We will define the target market towards which you want to focus your business. This market must have three key things: one is a need in the market that your product or service can satisfy; the second is easy access to your business; the third is an identification of the value of your service or product in exchange for the experience only you can provide. Your main target market can be defined through answering a series of questions based upon a set of criteria that help define your existing customer base in detail.

Geographic:

Where is your business located?

Do your customers have physical or virtual access to your business?

What area of expansion do you want to penetrate?

_____

_____

Demographic:

Your customers' age, sex, race, ethnicity, marital status, family size, life cycle.

Your years in business, its ownership, the decision-makers, the business cycle.

_____

_____

Socioeconomic:

Your customers' occupation, education, income.

Your goals in terms of sales, profits, marketing your business.

_____

_____

_____

Psychographic:

Your customers' lifestyle, personality, tastes.

Your corporate culture. The values and mission of your business.

_____

_____

_____

Behavior:

How do your customers act? What do they respond to? What are their likes and habits? What do they do?

_____

_____

My customers buy:
- What?
- When?
- Where?
- How?
- Why?
- How much?
- How often?

The benefit from defining your target market is that you are able to see the trends, groups and types more clearly in order to determine the best way to serve and grow your business. It is important to identify whether if your business is directly aimed at individuals or is focused on companies, because this determines how you should apply the tools we are presenting.

It is a question of all of the factors your customers take into consideration during the purchase process.

STEP 2: Second-level market

To determine the second-level market, it is necessary to be clear about the principal market. You can use various existing techniques for the development of ideas, such as brainstorming calls, mind maps, etc. Any of these techniques will allow you to open the creative field in your mind that is often not used during the routine of everyday life. Remember that you are the person who knows your business best; only you have lived through all the critical and noncritical moments of your business; you have experienced the birth and growth of your business, as well as its stagnation. All these experiences are valuable, because that way you know which roads you have traveled that have failed, as well as those that have been successful.

On the other hand, it is important that this plan be developed as a team. If you have staff within your organization in various areas and there are people you know who are not involved in the business, but have the spark of creativity, you can form a multidisciplinary team to generate business ideas for the second-level market. It is always important to value differences, because often when we work as a team and a member thinks differently from the others, the normal human reaction is to immediately reject that person's input and not to provide the opportunity to express an idea that the "typical group" may not have seen. Valuing differences is a fundamental principle for teamwork and the generation of creative ideas for businesses.

Once you have generated the potential and the prospects for the second level, you can apply the questions from the previous step, with which you can determine the behavior of this new level of customers and thus move to the next step.

We will present a schematic table that allows you to describe the information for steps two and three in a structured form.

Product Service	Client (Level1, Level 2)	Group Associations
Video games	Young 8-20 years old (L1)	
	Parents (L2)	Group of parents
	Coaches (L2)	Baseball Teams

STEP 3: Access to groups and associations

In the same way we used brainstorming tools to determine second-level customers, we can apply them in identifying groups or associations that will allow us to optimize effort. Think for a moment about how your current advertising medium works on one person and how much it is costing you to use this medium, in money as well as in time and effort. The idea is to optimize resources, to try to make your advertising reach masses and groups, and often this route will be more economical than the traditional way.

When you analyze what your customers do, what their habits are, how they feel before and after using your product or service, their expectations, then you should understand, you should feel that you are in their shoes; and once you feel this deeply, you can make the connection regarding how to relate to groups or associations.

There is a mental process that we must understand as business owners. It may sound strange at first, but later you will understand it. You feel that your business simply offers a good product or service that is within reach of your customer. That sounds good, it could cover any business and keep it in business; but if I say now that you should **see your customer as a potential business partner**, you could say at first that it is not possible, because your customer is not in business to sell goods or services of any kind. But this is the key to your business; when you see your client as a partner, then you can visualize the way to make alliances with groups or associations.

The following example illustrates how a change in viewing the client makes a business grow and attract great opportunities using minimal resources:

Carlos has a gym in a residential area north of the city. He decided to change his marketing strategy to attract more customers. He began to see his customers as partners, offering them a membership card that gives them discounts on their monthly fees if they bring new customers to the business. Additionally, he offered membership packages to corporate groups in which executives and employees get certain benefits if they enter into the association or group. He also generated lines of business directed at the elderly, retirees, and groups of therapists. In this way he created and duplicated an advertising campaign without having to spend a large amount of money for it, and he multiplied his business exponentially.

As you can see, the main point is to determine:
- The product package/service you want to promote.
- Who the groups or associations are.
- The method or way to reach these groups.

With these three clear elements, you can supplement the above table and thus have the information better structured in order to move to the last step, which is the development of the campaign.

You can then use the following table to develop your business.

STEP 4: Develop campaigns

To develop a campaign, you need the above information, in addition to a focus on a standard approach. In other words, as you develop the first advertising campaign focused on the first package of products/services for a given association, think about what might work for the second and third levels of your list in a way that simplifies your efforts and saves resources.

It is also important to consider communication methods and social media, for through these you can reach large numbers of people and groups, and in many cases they are free or inexpensive.

Another important element is to value the people, organizations and groups to which you are affiliated or that you must join. Participating in chambers of commerce and in industry, and attending events and training, allows you to meet people; and these connections also function as a means of marketing your business, as in the familiar expression "hit the street." It is important to use both electronic media and human contact.

A campaign can have different structures and designs. The way to prepare an advertising campaign is well-documented in books and on the Internet, but the interesting thing is to connect all the information in the tables above and put it into practice. Remember that an idea without action is nothing.

CAMPAIGN NAME		FREQUENCY			
DESCRIPTION					
INNOVATION					
GROUP / ASSOCIATIONS		CONNECTION			
BENEFITS	CLIENT		ORGANIZATION		
RESOURCE					
PROGRAM					
ACTIVITIES	RESOURCE	COSTS	START DATE	END DATE	

You can schedule your campaigns in periods, and in this way you will have a controlled program that you can keep track of over time, as you should be measuring the results the campaign produces as you proceed, taking measurements on the path and making adjustments. Remember that you will not create a infallible program; this program can be changed and can be adjusted as it is implemented, and this way you will not have the sensation of waiting until the end to see the results.

To make the road shorter, you already have an analysis of your product and of the path where you can direct it; now you will develop how you will do it, and put action and passion into the implementation.

Notes:

How to create a Foundation, which incorporates other International Standards such as: (ANSI Z97.1, ASTM-C1036, ASTM-C1048, ASTM-C1172, etc.)

The best way to establish an integration of systems management is establishing a management system basis, where other systems may overlap. Currently the structure of PDCA is the best known to establish management systems.

The Plan, Do, Check, Act stages of the standards were used as a basis for a road map with the final "destination" of multiples certification. However the road map involved more stages, going beyond the intended certification and already foreseeing how certification could more easily be maintained and including the difficult area of setting up measurable Performance Indicators in each of the areas related, quality, safety, environment, glass, etc.

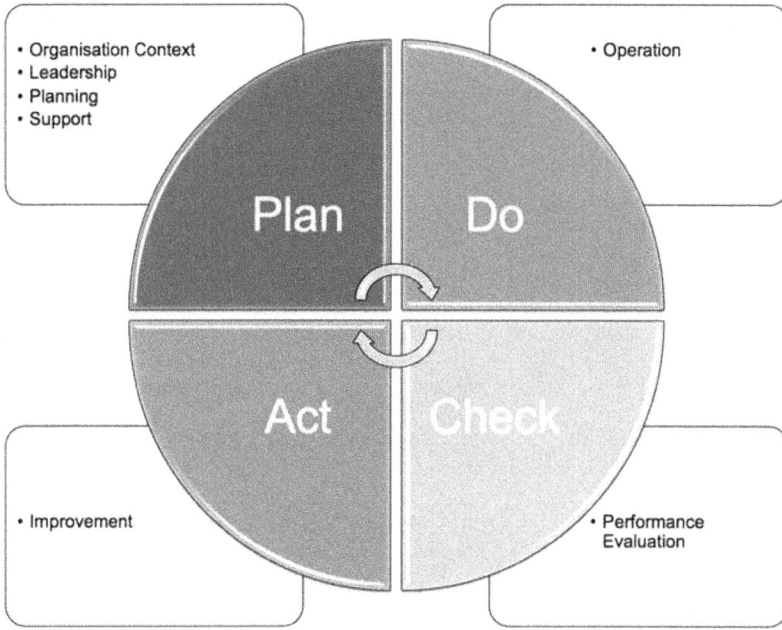

- Organisation Context
- Leadership
- Planning
- Support

Plan

Do

- Operation

Act

Check

- Improvement

- Performance Evaluation

PLAN	DO	CHECK	ACT
How to purchase critical material	Implement Quality & Environmental process	Evaluate the process by KPI and Internal Audit	Management Review process to improvement actions.
How document control will need to be managed	Document control procedure & Software	Evaluate the process by KPI and Internal Audit	Management Review process to improvement actions.

When developing and implementing an integrated management system it is important to establish common areas. These are the areas where the optimization of the management system allows the saving of resources and the efficiency of the system itself. When the system fully mature the organization can pursue a smart business.

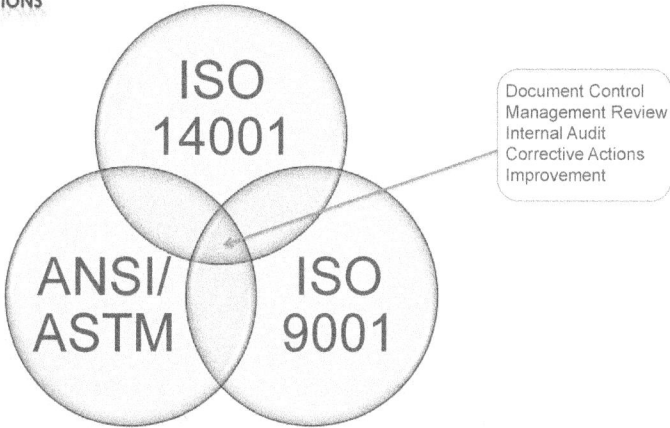

Document Control
Management Review
Internal Audit
Corrective Actions
Improvement

Notes:

Design Bridge from "Efficiencies/Cost" to "Innovation/Profit"

There are many ways of defining innovation, ranging from creating new inventions or new proposals to implementing them. It is said that an idea is truly innovative when it is designed and put into practice, and its benefits can be demonstrated. In order to generate innovation in your business you need to know the skills of your organization's members and the guidance and inspiration that the leader can offer.

When we speak of skills, they can be understood to be a reasoned knowledge for dealing with uncertainty; managing uncertainty in a world that is changing socially, politically, and in terms of labor in a globalized society in constant flux. Skills cannot be approached only as observable behaviors, but as a complex structure of attributes needed for performance in different cases where knowledge, attitudes, values, and abilities are combined with the tasks that must be fulfilled in certain situations.

Skills must be seen as complex processes that people put into action, performance, creation, to resolve problems and fulfill the activities of daily life and in the social, labor and professional contexts, contributing to the construction and transformation of reality. They integrate **the knowledge of being, the**

knowledge of knowing, and the knowledge of doing, taking into account the specific requirements of the environment, personal needs, and processes of uncertainty, with intellectual autonomy, critical consciousness, creativity, and a spirit of challenge. Skills consist of underlying processes, such as cognitive-affective processes.

Each person is a universe in dialogue with the world, so that a human is a differential sample, is the open and communicating result of the dynamic and interdependent complexity we live in; therefore, skills should be approached as a dialogue between three central axes: *the demands of the labor-business-professional market, the requirements of society, and the management of human self-realization.*

A skill is not an intrinsic characteristic or a separate question from the knowledge acquired through life experience. On the contrary, it is born and grows with a person, with the usefulness of the knowledge and the knowledge of its usefulness. A skill is a vehicle that transports knowledge, and intelligence is the lubricant that facilitates progress; both questions determine the level and performance of the final product resulting, ultimately, in the real skills of people throughout life. The formation of skills is a mixture of balanced forms where the most characteristic ingredients of knowledge try to discover some or many of the hidden flavors (talents, abilities, aptitudes, and attitudes) that have a major impact on your organization's resulting product.

Knowledge Management

Knowledge management is the learning and activity that allows you to generate, share, or distribute and use the tacit knowledge (know-how) and explicit knowledge (formal) found in a certain space, so that individuals and communities can apply it when they must meet their development needs.

Knowledge has always been considered a factor that promotes the advancement of civilization, and that allows us to solve problems, to adapt to environmental conditions, to manage groups, to impose rules, to face critical situations, and ultimately to improve the living conditions of humans.

At present, the need to increase the dynamics of change and to adapt to flexible working models has led to an increase in the intensive use of information as a key

resource for good performance. In turn, this fact increases the use of technology and the development of learning processes as a mechanism to incorporate new knowledge.

In the first case, a difficulty can arise with the incorporation of technology developed abroad or in other cultural contexts from differences between the cultural maturity of the place where it was created and that of the organization that wants to implement it, which translates into differences in practices. And in the second case, the failure to create a language for change in order to create learning of the new practices these technologies impose causes a consequent resistance to change.

Organizations must produce knowledge, even if acquired from outside; the need to prepare the adaptation of its members forces it to create objects of knowledge, such as transfer methodologies, conceptual models, the design of new skills, the definition of new processes, programs that administer learning and not training, design of fees for skills, study plans based on a skills approach, and the management of knowledge-based processes.

For organizations, knowledge management is the set of elements that describe a certain object or part of reality, which they use to act on this reality with greater efficiency and productivity. The elements range from neutral data, information, and knowledge applied to an object, acquired experience, and learned abilities, among others.

The process of constructing permanent knowledge involves active learning to work and to create these elements. In general, this process is generated in the same operative installed contexts and with a status quo that is prolonged in time. It does not involve the generation of adequate space for development and innovation, introduced into the operation, which generates noise and reasonable conflicts for those within the organization who are pressured by the daily production and the challenging effort to generate products and services with the constant changes in environment. Hence it is essential to manage a shared conceptual model which must be changed by the participants.

The volatility of the changes that take place in organizations in the context of the new economy, and the continuous introduction of new artificial intelligence technologies into production and management processes within organizations and companies, have in their turn provoked changes to organizational structures and even to the minds inside them.

The new labor realities are a big challenge and will be from now on; realities that have modified the labor relations contract between organizations, companies, and their members, with emphasis now placed on the development of people's knowledge.

It is not easy to give you immediate answers to this great challenge. Many companies or organizations have opted for the application of a system of labor skills, as an alternative to promoting training and education, in a direction that strikes a better balance between the needs of companies or organizations and their members.

People today are experiencing a process within a new frame of reference which comes from sustained technological development, especially in the new communication technologies, and from the new management models where the basic principles are: **learning to know, learning to do, learning to make, learning to live with others and finally learning to be**; this has a new significance for knowledge management as a new paradigm of the 21st century.

In the administrative context, the information society and the knowledge society are two dimensions of the ongoing process of development, in which human talents stop being passive subjects and become active participants, which facilitate the improvement of production processes and stimulate the introduction of new work skills to take on the most important and unique challenges of the current era, and overcome in this new way fears of failure, of rejection, of criticism, of the traditional patterns of hierarchy, and thus break old mindsets that have created so much damage inside and outside different organizations.

In this sense we can say that **knowledge** is the most valuable asset of any organization in the information society. Thus we speak of the knowledge society and knowledge economy. The competitiveness of firms, and therefore their survival, depends on this knowledge being preserved and used efficiently.

Hence, knowledge management can be seen as *the art of creating value from the intangible assets of an organization related to the use of strategic information to achieve business objectives, in order to perform an organizational activity that allows the creation of an infrastructure and social environment so that knowledge can be easily accessed, shared, and created, and is placed within the reach of every employee for your business to be effective.*

Work Culture

Work culture requires a new set of cognitive, social, and technological skills, since business organizations have adopted changes in at least two broad categories such as:

Networking. Pyramidal, hierarchical and closed structures have started to be replaced by interactive, open business networks, increasing the decentralization of decision-making to units that gain more autonomy. Central management assumes a role of defining strategies and evaluating results. The development of autonomy requires the acquisition of relational, organizational, cognitive, and technological skills.

Adaptability. This means that in organizations there has been a shift from the paradigm based on productivity, in which only standardization and volume are taken into account, representing a rigid model, towards a focus on quality, continuous innovation, and design. This leads to the notion of a factory that is flexible and adaptable to changing markets in terms of volume and specifications. In this context, the skills of adaptability, versatility and forming teams arise.

CONTINUOUS IMPROVEMENT

Competitive conditions mean that a modern company should be constantly changing. This implies that the new organization is conceived as a dynamic structure, identifying problems and seeking solutions. This translates into the need for a human resources policy that encourages _systematic training and creativity_.

These new conditions of productivity and competitiveness cannot be attained through limited and reduced training. This has led to substantial modifications to the concept and traditional practices of training, mainly in terms of content and the occupational levels catered to; and it produces a conceptual shift, which changes the relationship of education and training within the educational setting, not only at the university level but also at the business level. Organizations need to be clear about the new conditions of productivity that the business needs and align them with the training of its members.

Thus we need to develop policies for employment training that include the design and implementation of mechanisms that allow workers to better prepare themselves to play a role in a world of constant movement and new working conditions, which supposes the acquisition of basic skills or employability, obtained in formal education as well as corporate training based on practice and experience.

In this respect, we can affirm that the modernization of production based on the criteria of quality, efficiency, competitiveness, and productivity makes it difficult to change the approach from training programs focused on qualifying for a specific job. Certificates or diplomas obtained in this way are beginning to lose value, as what is becoming significant is not the ways in which knowledge was acquired, but the actual results achieved by individuals in their job performance.

In this sense we can say that knowledge management may be necessary to complement the formation of skills developed by members of the organization so that the business can manage its own processes, and can administer and provide services and products in a dynamic environment that easily adapts to market changes. In this way, a culture of continuous improvement is founded within the organization.

Continuous improvement as a culture

How can we create a culture of continuous improvement in which we can combine the production processes of the organization and the skills of its people? In our years of experience in the world of consulting, one of the most common strategies is to establish processes, procedures, performance indicators and audits, which with daily use create habits that then become organizational culture.

Continuous improvement of the effectiveness of the organization is based on the combination of the mission, vision, objectives, the results of management indicators, the analysis of data, corrective and preventive actions, risk control actions, the control of failures and complaints, and through internal communication processes among members of the organization such as: management review meetings; quality management meetings; operational results meetings; complaint meetings, in which the organization collects information about: measurement reports and data analysis; reports on the results of internal audits; external audit results (customers and suppliers); complaints about product and service quality; minutes of the various meetings; status of corrective, preventive and improvement actions; and reports on the results and effectiveness of actions taken.

At these meetings the organization should deal with the following: review of the behavior (effectiveness, efficiency, potential weaknesses, external effects, opportunity to use better methods, control of changes both planned and unplanned) of processes, and then a review of the different plans of action that have been established. Among the participants, the organization should identify opportunities for required improvement and evaluate priorities, in order to make a decision on the development of improvement projects. The actions arising from the evaluation of the processes responsible must be recorded, along with the names of responsible persons and the implementation dates. The information collected, as well as agreements made, will be input for the organization's continuous and infinite process of improvement and knowledge management.

For you to be able to create this team of creative, innovative people in an environment of continuous improvement we offer the following steps:

STEP 1: Keep track of all complaints, claims, and internal problems within the organization.

STEP 2: Use the "**Continuous Improvement**" form and place in the first column the name of the process that is affected by the problem you want to improve.

STEP 3: Determine the input data that affects the process and determine whether this is the data that can measure the problem.

STEP 4: Establish a team of people who will participate as an improvement group to help solve the case.

STEP 5: Determine the cause and possible alternatives for improvement; here you can apply various existing techniques for the identification of problems and their causes.

STEP 6: Determine what resources you need to implement the proposed alternatives.

STEP 7: Begin to perform the proposed actions and assess the impact of those actions.

STEP 8: Review and measure the effectiveness of actions and record it. If you find that the actions are helpful, continue doing them; if not, return to step five and again review the causes and new actions.

STEP 9: When you see that the problem is improving, document it, and connect it to daily processes as well as any internal training process that is required or should be established.

STEP 10: Periodically re-evaluate the situation to monitor its behavior.

Congratulations. Here you have completed the goal of the 90 days of challenges that have allowed you to bring all the elements together to develop a method of constant review, and in this way to establish a dynamic organization where changes and continuous improvements produce evolution.

CONTINUOUS IMPROVEMENT

PROCESS	INPUT	TEAM MEMBERS	CAUSE	ALTERNATIVES	RESOURCE	DATA MEASURE	MEASURE FREQUENCY	COMMENTS

www.ingramcontent.com/pod-product-compliance
Lightning Source LLC
Chambersburg PA
CBHW060632210326
41520CB00010B/1578